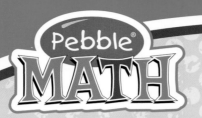

# It's
# Addition!

by M. W. Penn

Consulting Editor: Gail Saunders-Smith, PhD

**CAPSTONE PRESS**
a capstone imprint

Pebble Books are published by Capstone Press,
1710 Roe Crest Drive, North Mankato, Minnesota 56003.
www.capstonepub.com

*Library of Congress Cataloging-in-Publication Data*
Penn, M. W. (Marianne W.), 1944–
  It's addition! / by M. W. Penn.
    p. cm. — (Pebble books. Pebble math)
  Includes bibliographical references and index.
  Summary: "Simple rhyming text and color photographs describe addition"—
Provided by publisher.
  ISBN 978-1-4296-6038-9 (library binding)
  ISBN 978-1-4296-7069-2 (paperback)
  1. Addition—Juvenile literature.  I. Title. II. Title: It is addition! III. Series.
  QA115.P46 2012
  513.2′11—dc22                                                    2011003298

## Note to Parents and Teachers

The Pebble Math set supports national mathematics standards
related to algebra and geometry. This book describes and illustrates
addition. The images support early readers in understanding the
text. The repetition of words and phrases helps early readers learn
new words. This book also introduces early readers to subject-
specific vocabulary words, which are defined in the Glossary
section. Early readers may need assistance to read some words and
to use the Table of Contents, Glossary, Read More, Internet Sites,
and Index sections of the book.

Printed in the United States of America in North Mankato, Minnesota.
112012      007016R

# Table of Contents

# What Is Addition?

When you need to know how many,

Adding is the thing to do.

Count the total, find the sum:

Say "1 plus 1 equals 2."

$$1 + 1 = 2$$

$$4 + 1 = 5$$

6

# Add Two Numbers

Count 1, 2, 3, 4 fingers,

Then add in 1 thumb.

Hands together, 5 + 5,

And you find the sum.

$$5 + 5 = 10$$

You scored 2 big goals.

Your teammate scored 4.

Add the goals together

To find your team's score.

$$2 + 4 = 6$$

10

Oscar has 1 penny.

Mandy hasn't any.

Oscar's coins plus Mandy's coins

Equal just how many?

$$1 + 0 = 1$$

Mary Lou was 6 years old

And 40 inches high.

Then she grew 3 more inches,

And asked, "How tall am I?"

$$40 + 3 = 43$$

# Add Three Numbers

8 lemon drops in your jar.

Add 1 grape gumball

And 6 cherry lollipops.

How many in all?

$$8 + 1 + 6 = 15$$

$$1 + 4 + 7 = 12$$

The first mouse has 1 cheese chunk,

Plus 4 chunks for his spotted chum.

The third mouse has 7 chunks.

How many chunks for the sum?

7 red fire trucks.

3 yellow vans.

4 green convertibles.

Add them if you can.

$$7 + 3 + 4 = 14$$

# You Can Do It!

Count your fingers. Sum the score.

Add the cheese, then add more.

Find your height, add inches to it.

Add them all. You can do it!

# Glossary

**add**—to find the sum of two or more numbers

**equal**—the same as; an equal sign is shown as =

**plus**—to add something; a plus sign is shown as +

**sum**—the amount you get when you add two or more numbers together

# Read More

**James, Adele.** *Adding with Apes.* Animal Math. New York: Gareth Stevens Pub., 2011.

**Shaskan, Trisha Speed.** *If You Were a Plus Sign.* Math Fun. Mankato, Minn.: Picture Window Books, 2009.

**Steffora, Tracey.** *Using Addition at Home.* Math around Us. Chicago: Heinemann Library, 2011.

# Internet Sites

FactHound offers a safe, fun way to find Internet sites related to this book. All of the sites on FactHound have been researched by our staff.

Here's all you do:

Visit *www.facthound.com*

Type in this code: 9781429660389

Check out projects, games and lots more at
www.capstonekids.com

# Index

**Word Count: 187**
**Grade: 1**
**Early-Intervention Level: 15**

**Editorial Credits**
Gillia Olson, editor; Juliette Peters, designer; Sarah Schuette, photo stylist;
    Marcy Morin, studio scheduler; Laura Manthe, production specialist

**Photo Credits**
All photos by Capstone Studio/Karon Dubke, except: iStockphoto/kali9, 8 (top);
Shutterstock/leedsn, 8 (bottom)

The author dedicates this book to Ken, Bob, and Greg Novak and Joan Novak Harris.